THE
BRAVE KIDS

ADVENTURE
SERIES

VOLUME 1

DEDICATIONS

Praises God and my children Aaron, Candace, Chris, and Daaiyah. To all my family members that went on with the Lord. My sisters Toni and Sylvia. #1 fans, grandsons Tyrell, Justen, and Chris. The love of my life. Sal encourages me not to give up and keep striving to be the best. A special thanks to my extended family members at Southern New Hampshire University, mainly Mrs. R. Anderson.

Spiritual hugs to Fatimah, Connie, and Belinda, each of you made yourself accessible to straighten my crown and kept me polished whenever the crown became tarnished. Thank you everyone, for your support.

WELCOME TO THE BRAVE KIDS ADVENTURE SERIES

You must complete the adventures throughout the book to gain stars.

During the adventure, focus on the questions and then answer. Take your time.

It's not a race. It's all up to you. Are you brave enough to meet the challenge?

Once you exceed ten stars,

you will officially become a member of the Brave Kids Adventure Series.

Focus on each adventure and what you learned.

If you're ready for adventure, Let's go!

Contents

1.

2.

3.

Chapter 1

TELL YOUR STORY

Twelve-year-old twins Lacey and Casey enjoy their mile walk to and from school with their best friends, 11-year-old Jacob and 13-year-old Tim. Each day, someone from the group is selected to create an adventure because nothing exciting ever occurs in their small town of Shuttermout, Nebraska. Today is Tim's turn. The group asks, "What's today's adventure, Tim?"

Tim replied, "Grandma Susie's cookies."

Jacob replied, "Oh, here we go. Boy, just because you're chubby doesn't mean every story has to be related to food, Tim!"

Casey says, "Because of your cruel statement, Jacob, you must suffer whatever consequences Tim selects."

Lacey interrupted and said, "Jacob, you must first apologize. Friends are supposed to love one another unconditionally, not hurt the person you care about."

With his head hung low, Jacob apologized. Tim accepted his apology with a smile and said, "Jacob, the consequences of your actions, you must walk the rest of the way home with your shoes on the wrong feet."

Looking shocked, Jacob blurted, "Tim, we just started walking; that's a half mile of pain! My feet are going to be hurting the entire time."

Casey replied, "Your feet won't hurt as bad as Tim's feelings from your mean comment."

Question:

Remember to think before circling the answering

A. Did Jacob give Tim a compliment?

B. Was Jacob's statement mean?

C. Did Tim punch Jacob in the mouth?

The rest of the group chanted, " Take them off! Take them off!"

Everyone began to laugh as; Jacob sat on a log, trying to maneuver his feet in the opposite shoe. Lacey says, "Okay, Tim continue the story."

Jacob waddled like a penguin on hot coals as the group walked along the dirt road. Tim continues the story, trying hard not to laugh at Jacob.

"This adventure has a reward if you guys pay attention. Since my grandma's house is before we reach home, she suggested we stop past and enjoy cookies and milk. Grandma Susie made three dozen cookies. She made oatmeal, sugar, and double chocolate cookies. Just thinking about them makes my mouth water," Tim told them.

A. Should the group ask for a ride from the next car on the road?

B. Ignore the request and keep walking

C. Schedule the visit for another day with their parent's consent.

As the friends reached halfway home and Jacob slowly walked behind, a truck gradually approaches them. It's Deacon Wilson from church. He greets the children and asks, " If you guys need a lift home, I'm heading that way. I don't mind. You all can hop in the truck."

The children all said, "No, we're fine," including Tim even though his feet were killing him.

Deacon Wilson made the offer a second time and said, "Well, you guys get home safe. Oh, by the way, Jacob boy, maybe if you put your shoes on the right feet, you could walk faster."

Jacob replied, "Alright, thanks, Deacon. Have a good evening."

Question:

A. Did the friends get in the truck?

B. Did Deacon Wilson force the group into the truck?

C. Did the group thank Deacon Wilson but refuse the ride?

When Deacon Wilson drove off, Tim, Lacey, and Casey burst out laughing!

Jacob sat down for a minute to rub his sore feet. Tim encouraged the group to start jogging since he could see his Grandma Susie's house a short way up the lane.

Tim, Lacey, and Casey couldn't believe how ridiculous Jacob looked as he raced past them to Grandma Susie's house.

When Jacob arrives, he happily shouts, "I beat you all here! Ha, Ha!"

Jacob sat on the porch, rubbing his feet. When the group approached the house, Jacob noticed his friends walking past the house laughing. Putting his shoes back on the wrong feet, Jacob asked, "Tim, what's up? We're supposed to have cookies and milk at your granny's house.

Tim smiled and replied, "If you remember, Jacob, our parents trained us to stay together and come directly home from school. We're not supposed to stop anywhere without our parent's permission.

Yes, my grandmother did invite us to cookies and milk at her house, but the jokes on you! I never said the day or time of the visit. Since it's my adventure, I can change the story whenever I want."

Lacey and Casey began to applaud.

Casey said, "Thanks for creating a great learning adventure. Under no circumstance should we separate or take rides from people without our parents' permission."

Tim replied, "Safety ALWAYS comes FIRST! We must listen to our parents or guardians; that's how we gain knowledge."

Dear Reader:

What did you learn from the adventure?

Chapter 2
BEWARE!

Marcy Pagano and her daughter Tina were completing their Saturday morning cleaning routine. Marcy's music playlist echoed throughout the house as the pair cleaned. Unlike other teenagers, Tina enjoyed the Saturday routine because once the chores were complete, Tina and her mother could spend the rest of the weekend relaxing. By 11:15 am, Tina and Marcy were on their way to the supermarket.

Tina walked beside her mother in the market, observing her surroundings; she felt like someone was following them. As Tina bent down to tie her sneaker, a young girl bumped into her with her cart. Before Tina could address the incident, she heard a male voice say, "Little sis, pay attention; you bumped into the beautiful lady."

The girl appeared to be shaken up by the incident. The man and the girl repeatedly apologized.

Tina smiled slightly and replied, " I'm okay; no harm was done."

Tina quickly rushed in search of her mother. Marcy was in the checkout line. She asked, "Honey, where did you go?" Checking out her surroundings, Tina stated, I bent down to tie my sneaker, and a weird kid bumped into me with her brother's cart."

Marcy asked her daughter if she was alright.
Tina replied, "Yes, let's hurry home."

Question:

If Tina sees the pair again, what should she do?:

A. Ask for their name and address

B. Write a description of the pair

C. Invite them over for dinner

Once Tina and Marcy arrived home, they put the groceries away. Marcy said, "Honey, I'm too exhausted to cook. Could you order a large pizza and hot wings? I'm going to take a shower. The money's in my wallet on the table near the front door. Oh, also find us a good movie to watch. Thank you, sweetheart."

Thirty minutes later, the doorbell rang; viewing the porch camera, Tina could see it was the delivery man. Through the intercom, Tina asked how much the delivery was. The guy replied, "$27."

Tina opened the door and gave him $30. To her surprise, it was the guy from the supermarket.

With a broad smile, he said, "This must be fate. We meet again. My name is Mike. What's yours?

Tina angrily replied: " My Pizza!" Tina snatched the food from the delivery guy's hand and said, keep the change!" Tina quickly closed the door and locked it.

Question:

A. Should Tina tell the delivery guy her name

B. Should Tina tell her mother what occurred

C. Should she ignore the situation

When her mother came downstairs to eat dinner, Tina displayed the food on the T.V. trays. After dinner, the mother and daughter spent the rest of the evening relaxing and watching movies.

Early Sunday morning Tina was awakened by her mother. She apologized and said, "Tina, I'm sorry. We had plans for today, but unfortunately, the hospital is short-staffed, and I must go to work."

"It's okay, Mom. I'm just going to hang out at home. Is it alright if Bethany comes over?"

Her mom replied, "Sure, but first, let me check with Bethany's mother. I will call you around noon and let you know."

Tina replied, "That's cool, mom." Marcy glanced at her watch and said, I must go. It's 8:30 am. Could you lock the door for me, please? They embraced then Tina locked the door and went back to bed.

While Tina awaited her mother's call, she began organizing her clothes for the week. At 11:50 am, Tina received a text alert on her cellphone.
She noticed it was an unknown telephone number.

The text read, " I hope you're having a wonderful day, beautiful. "

Before Tina could respond, her mother sent a text stating Bethany was in Wildwood with her family and she wouldn't be able to visit.

Tina replied, " It's okay. I'll see her in school tomorrow."

When Tina was about to rest her phone on the nightstand, another anonymous text appeared, " Please don't ignore me. I had to jump a lot of hurdles to get your number. Seeing you each day at school takes my breath away."

Tina thought to herself, "Who IS this person?"

As if her phone could hear her thought, it pinged again.

"If you are wondering who I am, put your mind at ease. I'm your secret admirer, trying to find the courage to ask you on a date."

Tina replied, "Sorry, pal, I don't go out with strangers.

If you wanted to get to know me, you would unblock your number and have an actual conversation."

The individual replied, "I guess that can happen since you are home alone. Maybe you can invite me over, and we can finish watching the movie you fell asleep on last night."

Question:

A. Should Tina invite the caller over for a visit

B. Do you think the caller was a stalker?

C. Should Tina notify her mother immediately?

Frightened by the texter's response, Tina called her mother immediately.

She explained the details in the conversation and pleaded with her mother to hurry home.
Marcy instructed Tina to go directly to the panic room and take her phone.

The panic room was a small soundproof room hidden behind a panel in the hallway closet.

Once Tina entered the panic room, she locked the door. The cell rang. It was the stranger calling. Trying not to sound afraid, Tina cheerfully said, " Hello."

The caller replied, "I'm delighted to hear your voice finally. My name is Michael Brewster. Tina, you're unaware of this, but I'm your biggest fan.

If you open the front door, we can meet face to face. I brought you a bouquet of red roses."

Trying hard not to cry, Tina asks Michael to hold on because her mother was calling on the other line. He agreed. Tina gave her mother a quick update, and she included the caller's name. Marcy reassured Tina that she was safe if she remained in the panic room.

Marcy also stated, "Keep him talking because your uncle Wade is on patrol in the area. He and his partner are a few blocks away. Uncle Wade will text you when to answer the door, so he can make the arrest. I'm five minutes away. Please, honey, remain calm."

Tina agreed and clicked back to the other line. She stated, " Forgive me, Michael. I was trying to get my mother off the phone and change my clothes because I was wearing my pajamas."

Michael replied, " That's why I'm in love with you because you are so considerate."

Before Tina could answer, her uncle texted, "I see him at the door. Please open the door so we can arrest this clown!"

Tina rushed downstairs and slowly opened the door. When she did, her Uncle Wade slammed Michael against the wall and placed him in handcuffs.

Marcy arrived just in time to comfort her crying daughter.

Uncle Wade asked Tina, if she had seen him before. She replied, " Yes, several times. He delivered our food last night and, come to think about it, around my school and at the supermarket yesterday."

"He's a grown man who may have been stalking you for a while. Listen, I must go to the police station and complete the paperwork on his arrest. Marcy, the two you will need to the station to make a statement. See you guys later. Love you both."

Question:

When Tina and her mother entered the house, what did they talk about?

A. The recipe for s'mores

B. Who's Tina's favorite rapper?

C. Safety Methods

After returning from the police station, Marcy asked
Tina to think about what she could've done differently.

14

Question:

What do you think?

1. ....

   ....

2. ....

   ....

3. ....

   ....

Bonus star:

Describe three of the stalker's actions that frighten you
the most.

1. ....

   ....

2. ....

   ....

3. ....

   ....

Chapter 3
MR. PATRICK'S CLASS

Today was five-year-old Devin Duffy's first day at kindergarten. Devin was getting dressed as his mother, Lena, was preparing his lunch. She hoped the conversation Devin had with his father, Malcolm encouraged him not to cry when it was time for her to leave him at school.

After breakfast, Lena decided not to mention school since Devin was in a good mood.
She didn't want him to be nervous. The drive to school was twenty minutes away.

When Lena arrived, Devin opened the car door and shouted, "Wow! Look at all these kids!
I'm going to have so much fun."

Lena remembered her 8-year-old niece, Lia informed Devin the night before; she attended Lyons Elementary, and the children were friendly.

As Lena gathered her belongings, Devin requested, "Come on, Mom, let's find my teacher Mr. Patrick!"

Lena couldn't believe how Devin walked with such confidence. Once he approached the classroom at the end of the hall,

Devin yelled, "Mom! I found my teacher. He's the man whose picture is in my letter; that's Mr. Patrick."

Lena urged Devin to calm down because running and shouting through the hall was inappropriate behavior.

Mr. Patrick welcomed Devin and Mrs. Duffy to his classroom. Mr. Patrick gave Devin a name tag and escorted him to the snack table with his classmates. Upon his return, Mr.Patrick briefly explained the curriculum to Mrs. Duffy. Mr. Patrick noted Devin would bring home a folder containing classroom activities, homework, and a behavioral chart.

In addition, Mr. Patrick encouraged Mrs. Duffy to review the folder and sign Devin's homework and behavioral chart regularly. At the end of the meeting, Mrs. Duffy interrupted Devin's conversation to ask for a kiss goodbye.

When Mrs. Duffy puckered for a kiss, Devin whispered, "Give me a fist bump; I'm too old for hugs and kisses in front of people."

Devin's statement stunned Mrs. Duffy. She delivered a fist bump and quickly walked to her car.

Question:

What do you think happened when Devin's mother got in her car?

A. Did she burst into tears?

B. Did she go to work?

C. Did she drive to the spa?

When Lena got in the car, she burst into laughter because she couldn't believe Devin's new attitude. With the day off from work, Lena decided to treat herself to a spa day.

After two hours of relaxation, Lena felt rejuvenated. She thought, "Thank God I don't have to cook. I placed the roast in the crockpot this morning, and hopefully, it's done."

When Lena reached home, she could smell the aroma of food once she opened the front door. As she could tell, dinner was complete. With two hours left before Devin's arrival, Lena decided to set her alarm to take a nap.

She rested comfortably on the sofa; her alarm rang at precisely 3:00 pm.

Lena awoke and waited patiently sitting on the porch with a cup of hot coffee. At 3:20 pm, the bus pulls in front of Duffy's door.

When the bus doors open, with a big smile, Devin races up the stairs and says, "Hi, Mom! I must use the bathroom!"

Lena sat on the sofa, waiting for Devin to talk about his first day. He enters the room, kisses his mother, and asks about her day. Lena stated she went to the spa and then asked Devin about his day.

Devin said, " I made many friends today, mainly at recess. The snacks and lunch were good! The work was easy because you taught me most of the lessons at home over the summer. Here's my folder; you must look at each page and sign it.

Look, I received a gold star for doing well in penmanship."

Lena was informed earlier of the parent's obligation, but she allowed Devin to explain, so he could get into the habit of sharing school activities.

As Lena reviewed the folder, Devin stated, " Oh, I forgot to tell you something. My classmate, Jessica, wet herself today. I think she was embarrassed because Jessica began to cry when Mr. Patrick took her to the restroom.

I was puzzled because she had gone to the bathroom earlier with the group and didn't cry."

Lena replied that Jessica was probably embarrassed and that, hopefully, tomorrow, she will have a better day. "Did you use the restroom at school today?"

Devin replied, No, because my friend Byron said he doesn't like Mr. Patrick staring at him when he's using the urinal."

Question:

Do you think Lena should investigate Devin's accusations regarding restroom conduct?
Circle: Yes or No.

A week passed, and Devin continued racing to the bathroom when he got off the school bus. The strange behavior of not wanting to use the restroom at school worried Lena, so she decided to communicate her concerns to her husband. Maybe Devin would give him additional details about the situation. Once Lena told her husband Malcolm, he decided to take the day off from work and investigate why Devin wasn't using the bathroom at school.

As father and son sat eating breakfast, Malcolm stated: "I'm proud of you, son. When I examined your folder, I saw many gold stars. Keep up the excellent work. Hurry up, son; I might be driving you to school; mother has concerns about you not using the restroom at school, and I'm also worried."

Devin slowly dropped his head Malcolm stated, "Son, you don't have to be afraid of anyone.
I'm your father, and it's my responsibility to protect you, and I love you. Pick your head up and tell me what's happening at school."

With tears in his eyes, Devin stated, "Mr. Patrick said, "Even though we live with our parents, in school, we must follow his secret rules or we will be punished if we tell on him."

Enraged by Devin statement his father smothered his emotions in hopes of getting his son to provide additional details. As Malcolm wiped the tears from his son eyes, he asked him to continue. "Dad every time one of my classmates uses the bathroom Mr. Patrick likes to wash them up and take pictures of them in their underwear. I don't go to the bathroom because I don't want him touching me and taking pictures on his cellphone."

Malcolm kissed his son and said, "You are the class hero and I'm proud of you. No more worries, I will handle this, and you will be fine. Mr. Patrick is a bully and he's must be stopped."

While Devin was finishing his breakfast, his father went upstairs and shared the details with Mrs. Duffy. When she heard the news, Lena was so upset she began to cry. To console his wife Malcolm gently kissed and hugged Mrs. Duffy.

Malcolm stated, "I need you to call all the parents on the contact list. Tell them what's going on in Devin's classroom. Ask them to question the children about Mr. Patrick's inappropriate behavior. Also, I'm demanding a meeting with Principal Harris this morning."

Within 45 minutes 11 parents stated their children were victims of Mr. Patrick's bizarre behavior.

Question:

What should Mr. Duffy do next?

A. Should he call his Pastor?

B. Should he contact Devin's doctor?

C. Should he call the Police?

*If you answer this question correctly, you've gained two stars.

When Devin finished breakfast, Lena stated, "Devin, I got a call; there's no school today. Since I don't have to work, we're going to the zoo. Wash your face and hands, so we can get their early. Daddy will join us later. He has to take care of some business."

With a big smile, Devin replied, "Wow! That's cool, Mom!"

Once Devin washed his face, his mom told him to get into the car. As Mrs. Duffy and Devin drove off, Malcom called his friend, a police captain, and gave details of Mr. Patrick's conduct.

After the information was shared, Malcolm went to the school to meet with the Principal and other parents. To the parents' surprise Mr. Patrick had called out sick, and a substitute was teaching his class.

Upon the parent's arrival with their children, Principal Harris took statements from the students involved. The police were called to the school, and immediately a warrant was issued for Mr. Patrick's arrested. He was arrested for child molestation and child pornography.

After the arrest was made, the investigators from the Special Victim's Unit discovered that Mr. Patrick was fired from his last school for inappropriate behavior with several former students.

Everyone wondered how he was able to get a job at another school.

The next day, when Devin returned from school, he arrived without racing to the bathroom. He stated, "Mom, two important things happened today.

You're not going to believe it!"

Lena was aware of the news, but she wanted to hear it from Devin.

She asked, "What happened, son?"

"Mom, we have a new teacher because Mr. Patrick left. I like my new teacher, Ms. Mitchell. She takes us to the bathroom and stands in the hallway until we finish. I went to the restroom twice today."

Lena asked, "May I have a kiss and hug? I'm so proud of you son!"

Devin replied, "Mom, you can kiss and hug whenever you like, just not in front of people. I'm not a baby anymore!"

Question:

What did you learn from this adventure?

Chapter 4
WALK THIS WAY

During the Monday morning assembly at Philadelphia's Haven Elementary School, Principal Crawford introduced a video on child safety.

Since the kidnapping of Brandon Lewis, the detectives noted, witnesses recalled catching a glimpse of a tall Hispanic man with a kid getting into a white van.

Principal Crawford proposed the pupils accept an oath of safety to protect themselves from child predators.

Assistant Principal Bryson held up a sign with the school's new promise. He instructed the pupils to raise their right hand and pledge loudly: "No strangers, No secrets!"

When the children agreed, Principal Crawford ended the assembly by encouraging the pupils to get home safely and to remember their promises.

Since the abduction of Brandon Lewis, a student at their school, the Principal and faculty have been on a high security alert.

At 3:00 pm, the students had finished another school day. As cousins Justen and Chris walked out the school doors, Chris stated, "I'm glad that corny assembly is over!" Justen replied, "I don't know why you are complaining. You slept through the entire program. Principal Crawford provided great safety tips."

Chris sighed heavily and stated, "Since you are smart, name at least five safety tips."

Justen replied, " Cuz,my time is money. You must promise to buy me a bag of chips and a can of juice."

Chris replied, "No problem, I have five dollars. Start reciting what you learned, smart guy."

Without delay, Justen began:

"#1. Walk in the middle of the sidewalk or closer to a building. By following instructions, you will prevent predators from snatching and putting you in their vehicle.

#2. Never yell for help when you are in danger. Shout " Fire" repeatedly until getting an adult's attention. Once you have the person's attention, tell them a stranger is trying to kidnap you. Ask if the person could wait with you until the police arrive.

#3. No strangers, No secrets! If a stranger approaches, do not speak or answer any questions.

#4. Try carrying your book bag on one shoulder. It prevents the predator from lifting you from your book bag straps and kidnapping you. The reason is, it gives you time to break away and run.

Create a mental description of the person for the police. Example: What was the person wearing, the color of their vehicle, the license plate number, what did they look like, and if the predator has tattoos or scars?

#5. If a stranger tries to convince you to get into their car, run in the opposite direction. Example: If the person was driving north, you need to run south, Because the stranger may not have room or time to make a U-turn and follow you.

When Justen finished the task, he said, "Come on Chris, the store is at the corner on our way home."

After making their purchase, the cousins came out of the store. A stranger approached Justen and Chris. He asked, "Can the two of you help me? I need to move boxes into my new apartment. I will pay each of you $50."

Even though the money sounded tempting, the stranger's offer went against the school child safety promise. The cousins ignored the stranger, even when he offered Chris and Justen dinner and dessert.

Noticing that the boys weren't interested, the man walked back to his van and drove away. Unbeknownst to him, Chris had taken pictures of the license plate and the color of the van with his cell phone.

Question:

What should Justen and Chris do next?

A. Go back into the store and purchase more snacks

B. Order a pizza

C. Go home and tell their parents and have them call the police

Justen and Chris shared the incident with their Uncle Aaron. Enraged by the incident Aaron stated, "That's possibly the dude who abducted your classmate."

Justen replied, You probably right, Uncle Aaron. Pacing the floor and cracking his knuckles, Uncle Aaron started, "I'm sure of it! I hope the police find him before I do."

Chris chuckled and challenged, "Uncle Aaron, what would you have done if someone kidnapped Justen and I?"

Their Uncle Aaron laughed and replied, "I wish him luck and hope he has a good job."

With the look of disappointment, Justen replied, "Why would you say that?"

Uncle Aaron replied, "Because the way the two you eat, the kidnapper would NEED a two good jobs!"

Chris burst into laughter and said, "Justen, it was a joke! Seriously what would you do?"

Uncle Aaron lifted his shirt displaying his abs and big fists; he stated,

"I would've crushed him with one punch!"

Justen chuckled and stated, " Oh boy, get ready; Uncle Aaron's about to share one of his Army adventures."

Uncle Aaron stood from his chair, standing '6 7" and weighing 289 pounds, and quickly lifted Justen from the sofa with one hand.

Justen shouted, "I was joking; put me down, please!"

Uncle Aaron replied, "Okay. Back to my story. I'm a military veteran; we only use weapons, when it's necessary. My hands are lethal weapons boy! If anybody ever hurt my family, I'm dropping the body off at the mogue."

Chris giggled and said, "The End. Come on, Justen, let's play a video game."

As the cousins played in the den, awaiting their parent's arrival, Chris said, "Justen, I'm glad you shared the safety tips with me because the $50 for the moving boxes sounds good. We could've eaten cheesesteaks for a week. If you weren't present, I likely would have gone with him. Cousin, you probably saved my life." Justen hugged his cousin and said, "I couldn't imagine life without you."

The next day, as Chris and Justen were walking to school, the man in a white van appeared and drove near them.

He stated, "It's drizzling this morning; why don't the two of you get in the van? I'll give you a ride to school."

Justen and Chris ignored the man again. The man yelled, "I know you heard me. Just let me park my van so I can speak directly to you."

When Justen heard what the man said, Chris asked, are you ready, Justen? He nodded his head and shouted, "Let's go! Run, cousin!" The cousins began to run. Chris continued, "Don't stop until we get to school!"

Side by side, the boys ran. When they saw the school was a half block away. Justen and Chris increased their speed. Gasping for breath, Justen said, "We got this cousin; we're almost there!" The cousins could hear the guy beeping his horn from a distance.

Once Justen and Chris reached the school, the cousins ran directly to the principal's office.
Principal Crawford asked, "What's wrong? Why are the two of you short of breath? Sit down while I get the two of you a bottle of water."

After a few sips of water, Chris and Justen began to share their story. When they finished talking, Principal Crawford angrily declared, we're going to get that creep today. I'm going to call the police."

Chris said, "I have a picture of the guy's van and license plate on my phone. Do you want to see it?"

Principal Crawford replied, "Yes." She took the phone to assistant principal Bryson's office.

She requested he copy the photos from Chris's phone and includes Brandon Lewis's image, then circulates the flyer throughout the community.

Assistant Principal Bryson responded, "I'm on it!"

While he rushed to complete the assignment, the police captain Clarence arrived to interview Chris and Justen. As the captain was speaking to boys He received a signal to call the station; Captain Clarence stepped into the hall to answer. Once he returned, Captain Clarence bellowed, "We got him!" Everyone in the office began to applaud.

With tears running from her eyes, Principal Crawford embraced the boys and declared, "I announced to all of you we were going to catch that creep today and we did! Chris and Justen, do you realize that the both of you are Haven Elementary School heroes?"

Captain Clarence asked to use the phone; Principal Crawford, told him that he could use the phone in her office.

As the news traveled throughout the school that the child predator was apprehended, the office began filling students and faculty.

Suddenly rushing out of Principal Crawford's office, Captain Clarence asked for silence because he had an announcement.

He shared, "The predator was arrested on Kelly Drive while eating lunch in the van, but the good news doesn't end with his capture! Brandon Lewis was found alive inside the van! He appears to be safe, but for safety reasons, Brandon needs to be examined by a doctor before being released to his parents."

The sounds of cheers were deafening. Principal Crawford stated, "Finally, there's good news to broadcast for the City of Brotherly Love! Justen and Chris, your attention to yesterday's assembly followed Haven Elementary School's motto: No Strangers, No Secrets! It should echo through every school to keep our children safe.

I'm proud to be your principal because the two of you made the city of Philadelphia look great today!"

Throughout the day, Chris and Justen were the talk of the school district. In addition, they became the talk of Philadelphia after everyone viewed their interview on " Good Morning Philadelphia!"

After the dismissal bell rang, Justen and Chris chuckled about the day's events as they walked home from school. Chris said, "You know I ran faster than you this morning; the predator was after us."

Justen replied," Boy, you'rme crazy! I wasn't just running fast because dude was chasing us. Man, I needed to urinate. I knew, if I relieved myself, it would stain my khaki uniform pants. That's why I rushed to the restroom before Principal Crawford returned with the water bottles." Chris didn't reply because he was laughing so hard.

Weeks later, during another assembly, there was no way Chris was going to sleep through the program because the cousins were being presented with the "Good Citizens Award" from Captain Clarence.

Earlier Chris and Justen accepted the awards; Principal Crawford stated she had a special guest who would like to share a special message. She declared openly, "Haven Elementary give a round of applause to one of our own, Brandon Lewis!"

The students commenced shouting Brandon's name in unison. As he stood in front of the microphone, Brandon was so overwhelmed with emotions; tears rolled from his eyes. When the cheers stopped, Brandon said, "I want to talk to you today about listening to your elders. Raise your hand if your parents have said, "Don't speak to strangers or take anything from a stranger. If I were sitting in the audience, I would raise my hands also. Even though I knew the child safety rules, I broke ALL safety rules because I felt like I was invincible. Nobody would kidnap me. I was a kid from the hood. Boy, I was wrong! A child predator snatched me by the straps of my bookbag and threw me into his van. For six days, I cried and begged him to take me back to my family.

If you missed the evening news report, let me tell you my entire story. When the police captured the child predator, they also found his human shopping list of the amount children he planned to kidnap. The list noted three boys and seven girls. If the goal were completed, the children would have been sold to child traffickers over the internet in other countries, never to be seen again. Please, listen to me.

We don't know everything as children, but if we listen and stay focused, we can protect ourselves from predators.

Thanks for listening to me.

Remember, "No Secrets! No Strangers!"

The students gave Brandon a standing ovation. Principal Crawford dismissed the students at the end of day.

As the author of " The Brave Kids Adventure Series, Volume 1," this story ends as I begin to write volume 2.

Read an important message on the next page.

Now that you have reached the end of "The Brave Kids Adventure Series, Volume 1," do you recall reading the introduction? The goal was to answer questions in the story, hoping to earn stars to become a member. Because of your hard work and determination, I decided not to calculate stars.

You have earned all the stars by finishing the book.

Congratulations!

You are officially a member of the Brave Kids Adventure Series!

The knowledge you've achieved makes you a star! Please don't allow anyone to darken your shine.

BEFORE YOU CLOSE
THE BOOK

I have several things to read each day:

1. I am a star! I must stay in a positive light to maintain my shine.

2. Listen to my parents, guardians, and elders; they hold the key that opens the door to wisdom.

3. No Strangers! No Secrets!

4. Children shouldn't have secret adult friends.

5. Don't keep secrets that make you feel uncomfortable.

6. If someone touches you inappropriately or says something inappropriate, shout STOP! Immediately tell your parents, a family member, or a school counselor.

If you continue following these lessons, you will shine brighter!

I know this seems like a lot to remember, but if you read these words of encouragement daily for a month, you will memorize them and won't have read them.
I must go now.

Hey! Drop me an email. Tell me what you liked about the book.

Start a fan club and receive a free autographed gift.

Sincerely,

Darlene L. Scott

Email address: authordlscott@gmail.com